Wild Notes

*Observations over time about birds
and other fleeting things.*

Mike Lubow

Published by Birdwatcher Books
Copyright © 2015 Mike Lubow
All rights reserved.
ISBN: 1499624468
ISBN-00: 978-1499624465

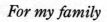

For my family

"*Beyond the wall of the unreal city... there is the old true world of the deserts, the mountains, the forests, the islands, the shores, the open plains. Go there....*"
— *Ed Abbey*

"*The creek runs on all night... whether I know it or care, as a closed book on a shelf continues to whisper to itself its own inexhaustible tale.*"
— *Annie Dillard*

Table of Contents

Introduction

Bird watching is a wilderness adventure enjoyed by rough and ready men and women, young and old.

You can be hard-muscled, hard-bitten, bug-bitten explorers who bushwhack the trackless wilds.

Or you can be ordinary folk who stroll neighborhood nature trails. Whichever, you're stalking wild animals, wild possibilities.

The animals could be spring migrants newly arrived from a South American jungle. Or winter vagrants that crossed a tundra to visit your neck of the woods.

You often get more out of bird watching than sightings. You get insights that would never have occurred if you hadn't decided to watch things that fly in and out of your life.

The jottings on these pages are an example of one regular guy's experiences with this. Sightings are reported. Ideas are, too.

Throughout "Wild Notes" the date shown on the left page indicates a true moment in time. The right page explains what happened then: what was seen and thought about. What was worth remembering and sharing.

When you get interested in birds, or anything ranging so freely outside of your daily world, you never know what you'll discover. Or where.

Sunday, May 31

Carry on

The Illinois forests were as thick and green as expected on the last day of May.

But the birds of summer didn't expect wind chills in the thirties and daytime highs in the forties. With a gusty north wind.

Scarlet Tanagers, Tree Swallows, Phoebes and Great-crested Flycatchers, Red-eyed Vireos, Kingbirds, Yellow-billed Cuckoos and a bunch of other seasonal visitors got their feathers ruffled by unusual weather.

Unusual weather has become usual. Maybe the birds understand, maybe they don't.

Either way, with an enviable indifference to that which is beyond control, they go about their business. There are irrevocable rules imprinted in the avian soul, and these get followed.

Sing for a mate, look for bugs to eat, start the nesting business. Ignore the guy with binoculars who's wearing a hooded jacket, ignore the wind and cold.

Carry on.

Tuesday, March 17

A goose on ice

A man looks at a Canada Goose on ice, and the man thinks…

If you're that goose, you're home. You know the smell and taste of it. You expect water to be here by now, not ice.

Green-brown, fishy water. With mud near the shore where your feet sink as you walk onto land to eat weeds that are as familiar as family.

This is the only place you want to be. But, the pond water that's in your blood, that should be rippling under you at this time of year, remains frozen.

Still, where else is there? This is where you, your brothers and sisters were born. Where your parents taught everything.

There's no question about where to be. You belong here, even though it's hard.

The wind is cold and the ice under your feet is lifeless as rock. You're a goose on ice. With a past, a place and a purpose.

So you wait. While that man over there watches, his hands in his pockets, shoulders hunched, hair blowing in the wind. He'll go away. You'll stay.

Friday, January 16

The unexpected

You think you know about birds, and then a bunch of Mourning Doves reminds you that maybe you've got something to learn.

Due to lazy thinking and a hazy memory, you figured these soft symbols of peace wouldn't stick around during the rough parts of a northern Illinois winter.

We've had sub-zero temperatures here, and frost-biting winds. You expect hard-ass woodpeckers and polar juncos to tough it out. But, doves were unexpected.

You go online to check the facts. Sure enough, maps on serious birding websites show that Mourning Doves have a year 'round range well within the edge of your area.

You didn't expect that. But the unexpected is always to be expected. Another bit of wisdom that comes from watching the birds.

Sunday, November 23

The upside down bird

The nuthatch is an asymmetrical bird. Big head. Little rear end. Which makes you think. Maybe it was shaped by the pull of gravity.

See, nuthatches spend most of their time upside down.

They creep down trunks that way. They eat seeds on your feeder that way. They look you in the eye that way. Your smile could be a frown to them.

The White-breasted Nuthatch is always worth a watch because it's less common than chickadees and juncos.

And also because, if this theory is right, its insides have dropped through the bird over time to enlarge its downward pointing front end.

Okay, it's a nutty theory to have hatched. But the bird's shape invites speculation on a cold, quiet morning.

We can be pretty sure that nuthatches think they're fine looking, and would tell us where we can put our ideas about asymmetry.

Still, next time you watch one, see if you don't wonder that maybe gravity had a hand in designing this bird.

Sunday, July 13

By the 4-lane

There's a dead tree near a 4-lane with a muddy pond and condos in the background. Not a snapshot of nature at her best.

Still, every year this tree is home to Double-crested Cormorants. Tropical birds that look out of place and out of time.

Why do they return? Why not go someplace away from car exhaust?

This makes you think about the power of "place" in our lives. Hell, I grew up in Chicago and still live there for no other reason than it's where I live.

The cormorants make you think of other things, too.

They reminded me of an essay by Ed Abbey, "Watching the Birds: The Windhover," in which he describes a tree where generations of vultures always return.

I re-read that essay because I noticed the cormorants and they reminded me of it. I'm glad I did. Abbey's writing delivers.

All because I saw cormorants while speeding on a 4-lane. No stopping. No binoculars, no hiking, just a glance.

If such a sighting makes you think about things, well, that's just one more reason bird watching is an interesting pursuit, even on days when it's not a rugged one.

Sunday, June 1

The Plover

Many years ago, I saw a Golden Plover while I jogged on a Hawaiian beach. I didn't stop to look.

I was interested in the sunshine, the waves, and there were all these bikinis around.

Turns out, the glimpse of that somewhat rare bird has been my only sighting of it.

If I saw one of these long-distance flyers today, I think I'd want to spend a little time watching it.

But that's not the way it happened.

This makes me recall words from a novel by Jim Harrison. In "Farmer" he has an old man say with some regret, "I still remember a girl I didn't talk to twenty-five years ago."

A passing observation from a book I read many years in the past. Some things, you just don't forget.

Thursday, February 6

Lost summer

Winter has been brutal.

Cardinals, woodpeckers, juncos, sparrows, nuthatches, jays and others are poking through snow-covered ground for seeds.

Some birds have snow on their heads. It coats their feathers. These cold birds don't care. They're all business, brisk business. Maybe, when summer comes they'll relax.

But, what if it doesn't come?

In 1816, it didn't come. That year, summer took a summer vacation. You can look it up. North America, Europe, the whole world, lost a whole season.

There was snow in June, frost in August. Crops failed. People moved. Skies were sunless and cold. In England, Mary Shelley got so depressed about it, she wrote the dark novel, "Frankenstein."

But our serious, snowy birds aren't depressed, and they aren't thinking about summer. They're thinking only this: one seed at a time, one day at a time.

They don't have time for the future. Today is all there is.

Friday, January 24

A thousand times

I took the picture years ago. I think I've looked at it a thousand times. It's of a doe staring back while trying to hide. But the tree she stands behind is skinny, and she isn't.

I keep the photo in my workout room, and smile at it every day while doing leg stretches against the wall where it hangs. It just doesn't grow old.

This gets me wondering about why we stay interested in the same things. Why we do something a thousand times.

I saw an American Kestrel on a wire. I pulled off the road onto a snowbank, got my binoculars, and looked. The hawk looked back, saying with penetrating eyes; "What you lookin' at?"

I thought it could just as well have been saying "What you still lookin' at'?"

Because I've seen a thousand Kestrels. After the first, you have lost your Kestrel virginity. But you don't have to lose your interest.

Maybe some day I'll quit looking at the same things. Quit doing the same things. Quit the same job. Maybe quit this writing.

Maybe not. After all, what's better than doing something a thousand times? Doing it a thousand and one times.

Monday, January 6

No compromise

Bird watching might've started as a compromise. As a kid you'd have preferred lions, crocodiles, gorillas.

But in the prairies and backyards near Chicago's steel mills you didn't get lions. Just birds

You saw a rare Purple Gallinule. That started it. Then Ring-necked Pheasants. And herons. Migrating wood warblers, too, although screw their picky little names.

You got Red-tailed Hawks. Barn Owls in dark alleys. You saw a Scarlet Tanager, a tease from the tropics in town for a visit. Turkey Vultures hung over the municipal dumps on that far south side of town. And a Bald Eagle, once in a blue moon.

You figured that if you ever went on a safari, you'd watch the real wild things. Hyenas, cheetahs, pythons. And you'd put birds on the back burner.

Now, you see it differently. It's a fierce twelve below zero, and your yard's full of beasts. Cardinals, Blue Jays, Fox Sparrows, Dark-eyed Juncos, Red-bellied Woodpeckers, Downy Woodpeckers, Mourning Doves, White-breasted Nuthatches.

Watching them might've started as a compromise, but it's not like that anymore. These guys are fierce. Hell, it's twelve below, and for them it's just another day on the job.

Saturday, December 14

Odd

There are trees in front of a suburban office building. They're leafless, but have red berries.

A flock of Cedar Waxwings has found them. You sit in your car and watch from the warmth behind your windshield. In addition to the novelty of waxwings, you see the oddity of flock behavior.

The birds are eating berries, or just squinting into the wind, freezing their butts. Then, bam, all take off, only to regroup a minute later.

Seems the flock has a mind belonging to it alone, not any one member. You think: whose idea was it to take off? Then to circle around and come back? Why did the others follow that guy? Or was there even one guy?

Maybe the flock itself is the one guy.

Flocks behave as though they have a central nervous system. Science has studied this, and come up scratching its itchy scalp.

You shake off these thoughts and leave the car. Time to go into the office building and observe another kind of flock behavior.

Sunday, November 24

Mars

This morning, real life looks like a still photo. I'm by a pond. Barely sunup. The sky's reddish behind the trees.

The pond is flat ice. I don't mind the cold, the quiet. Or the emptiness. But usually, there's something moving.

Juncos in the leaf litter. A squirrel. Once I saw a coyote on a morning like this, exhaling smoke. Now, nothing.

This must be what Mars is like. I wanted to go there when I was a kid reading science fiction. Today: screw Mars and its lifelessness.

We've got all the lifelessness we can handle, right here on this planet, on this pond, on this morning.

Then, wait. A bird flies from treeline to treeline. A familiar profile, a familiar wingbeat. An American Robin. Robins used to be our signal that warm weather was coming after a long winter.

Today, it's the only movement by a frozen pond at the start of winter. The irony is interesting. But it doesn't make this place less bleak. Well, maybe a little.

Friday, November 15

Soaring

Recently, a friend went paragliding off a mountaintop. Said there was a vulture nearby in the sky. They shared an updraft.

This reminded me of Ed Abbey, who praised the Turkey Vulture, a bird that "…contemplates our little world from a most serene and noble height."

In his book of essays, "Down the River," Abbey wrote that if there were reincarnation, he'd like to come back as a Turkey Vulture.

Not a bad idea. You have to admire a free-wheeling vulture, observing everything, threatening nothing, powerful, but not in the business of hurting, surviving on ready-to-eat food.

But a vulture's diet isn't worth dwelling on. The lazy soaring, now that's the thing. Might be nice to own the sky like that. And for a moment, I thought: gotta look into doing some paragliding.

Then I thought: …maybe not. Strapping on a parachute and helmet, dealing with the harnesses, buckles and belts—eh, I don't know.

Guess I'll stay down here and admire the Turkey Vulture's natural soaring. Just like I admire Ed Abbey's natural writing.

Saturday, November 9

Eye contact

Most contact with wild things is interesting. But eye contact is personal.

I was reminded of this when a friend sent me a photo of a bear taken in a relative's backyard. The animal's frank gaze reminded me of a few experiences with stares.

In the woods recently, thought I was alone. Then I noticed a coyote standing not far, watching. His brown and gray colors blended into the November trees. We made eye contact, and held it.

Then he'd had enough, and trotted off.

Near an icy pond last year I saw a Great Blue Heron. He turned to look down his nose at this guy with the noisy boots. We locked eyes. After a while, I hiked on.

And once, in a forest near Lake Superior, it was just me and my old camera on an empty trail. Or so I thought. Then a big-bellied guy holding a hunter's slingshot came out from behind a tree. We made eye contact.

But we broke it, and went our separate ways. The bear made me think of all that.

Sunday, October 27

Mad at the woods

From your car on the way to work you see a Blue Jay. Juncos. A Yellow-rumped Warbler. You're not even on a hike. You ditch work and head to the woods.

No birds. Nothing. Just a lot of empty trees and fallen leaves. The leaves crunch when you step on them. You get a little mad. Mad at the woods.

Wait: that's crazy. The woods didn't do anything. They're just being what they are, with or without birds. Quiet trees, noisy leaves.

And the woods don't care that you're mad. They don't need you in them. Birds don't need you there. You ditched work, and the woods couldn't give a rat's ass.

This makes you mad at yourself, and the woods, too. You cut your losses and hike out.

As you near the trailhead you see a Turkey Vulture. He's looking down on you. You figure he's thinking that if you don't cool off you might become a nice meal.

This makes you smile. But, just because you're smiling, doesn't mean you're going to forgive the woods. They don't get off that easily.

Sunday, October 20

But...

You have a hands-off philosophy about nature. You say: Don't cull suburban deer, don't trap coyotes, don't chase off geese and crows; don't hire an animal removal guy to get rid of a beaver.

This is how you feel while sitting on a log, deep in the woods by a riverbank. But...

Yeah, but. Here's a 'but' you didn't see coming. Back home, a skunk moves in under your house. It's a four-legged tear gas canister, and its smell gets in every room.

You remember a picture you saw in an old bird book: a Great Horned Owl had caught a skunk. The owl's huge talons pinned it against a tree limb, and the owl was about to dig in.

Maybe you felt a little sorry for the skunk, skewered that way.

But...now, as you air out the house you're thinking: screw the skunk. Screw your hands-off philosophy.

You're gonna have to look up that animal removal guy. Unless a Great Horned Owl gets over here and starts doing his job.

Wednesday, October 9

Tale of two trees

There's a big apple tree nearby. Many of its apples have dropped as they do this time of year.

The fallen fruit used to attract bees. You had to watch your step. You could get stung. But, there are no bees now.

There's another big tree not far from here. Unlike the apple, it's dead. Branches look like claws. And it's full of cormorants, a whole colony.

Cormorants used to be uncommon. Your neighbor would say—hey, look, a vulture. Privately, you'd think: nope, that's an odd bird called a Double-crested Cormorant.

This fall, you've got these two trees to wonder about.

One's alive and full of fruit, but uncommonly free of bees. The other is lifeless, and uncommonly full of cormorants.

Once, our part of the world had many bees and few cormorants. What's going on? That's up to science to figure out, if it can.

Meanwhile, the common old thought hits again: change happens—get used to it.

Thursday, October 3

Leave it to beaver

A beaver's chewing trees around the lake. Homeowners want to chip in and hire a trapper.

One neighbor says: hell no. He moved here to be around herons, geese and ducks, sandpipers, tanagers and thrushes, owls, deer, muskrat, skunk, possum, raccoon, mink, coyote, fox, snakes, and if need be, beaver.

He gets outvoted. A trapper soon catches a 40-pound beaver, befuddled in a cage.

The dissenting neighbor won't pay his share of the trapper's bill, causing dissent. But why should he pay?

One answer: democracy rules. Second answer: ever hear about the "tyranny of the majority?"

You feel bad for the neighbor, bad for the lost trees, bad for the beaver. What to do? Go bird watching.

Later, deep in the woods where trees naturally live or die, a woodpecker hammers in the distance.

You search for it, moving further away from people and the complications of democracy.

Wednesday, September 11

Time

My son reminded me that we'd argued years ago about rushing to get him a fast-food meal advertised as a limited time offer.

I never liked limited time offers.

Went into the wild to clear my mind. This doesn't always work. The quiet woods can be a philosophy classroom if you're not careful.

The thought hit that Scarlet Tanagers are a limited time offer. I missed mine this summer.

Hell, it doesn't stop with birds. Sunday's NFL game had a former player doing analysis. He looked nothing like the jock we remember. He looked like my wife's Uncle Louie.

Even the blond bombshell who sings the NFL theme song got replaced by a younger blond bombshell. Face the music: we're all limited time offers.

It took a Great Blue Heron to get my mind off this stuff.

We stared each other down. He was unflappable. We know he won't stay when ice comes. But his eyes said he doesn't give a crap about limited time.

Gotta be more like him. While there's time.

Thursday, August 22

Seventy percent

Low clouds, steady drizzle. This Midwestern wildlife preserve has the feel of a rainforest. Heavily overgrown, shadowy and damp.

There are no birds. That's okay. It's August. It's raining. You don't expect birds.

You walk through a clearing and notice a broken, wooden fence. Years ago, on a day that wasn't gloomy like this one, you saw a meadowlark sitting there in sunlight. You remember things like that.

You also remember reading recently that Eastern Meadowlarks have declined by 70% in the last few decades.

Today, this wilderness preserve makes you think of the famously endangered rain forests we hear so much about.

But it's nothing like them. It's just a nature preserve on a rainy day.

Still, the thought hits: was that meadowlark the last one you're going to see around here?

Friday, August 16

The desensitized bird watcher

C'mon. A common Cardinal is a knockout.

It's not officially called a "common Cardinal." It's officially known as a Northern Cardinal. But just the same, it's pretty common.

Actually too common, and that's the problem. You see one at the side of the road or in the bushes next to your kitchen window and you don't give it a second thought.

But wait. Give it a second thought.

If this bird were rarely seen, like, say, a California Condor, a Painted Bunting, a Pileated Woodpecker, a Golden Eagle, a European Goldfinch in an American meadow…it would stop traffic.

Not just because it's got a pyramid-shaped beak, a black-patterned face, a long tail, a sharply pointed crest, but because IT'S ALL COMPLETELY BRIGHT RED.

So why the apathy toward Cardinals? Answer: they're "common Cardinals." You see them every day. You are Cardinal desensitized! See if you can figure out a cure for this.

Friday, August 2

Wanderlust

In the woods, you see a Phoebe. Reminds you of a dog named Phoebe. Good times.

Further down the trail: coyote scat. Reminds you of studying coyotes and collecting this in baggies which you kept in the freezer until your wife threw it out, and almost threw you out.

Okay—focus. You lean against a tree—best way to see birds. But ants climb aboard, and you do a little dance.

This reminds you of dance lessons reluctantly taken before a wedding. Couldn't get the hang of it. C'mon. Clear your mind.

The effort to stop random thoughts reminds you of Zen. This reminds you of championship coach Phil Jackson. Which reminds you of basketball. Maybe you'll shoot some hoops later.

Then you see an Eastern Kingbird in a clearing. A rare bird only because all birds are rare in the August quiet. But it reminds you of a comment from a nun in Dakota.

She saw an Eastern Kingbird next to a Western Kingbird on a wire. Eastern sat east and Western, west. A damn cool observation, but she didn't say damn.

You go wandering and you might find birds. Your mind goes wandering, and who knows what it'll find. No matter, you gotta go wandering.

Wednesday, July 24

A lot of bird

You don't see a lot of birds in midsummer.

Today, it was midsummer with a vengeance. Quiet. Just sun and bugs. Trees heavy with green. Tall grass in the prairie.

But there was a Red-tailed Hawk circling overhead. Like a kid with arms outstretched pretending he's an airplane.

It wasn't hunting. When hawks hunt they drop from a branch onto a squirrel. Or dive in fast to grab a duck. No, he was doing what he was doing just because it was fun.

Maybe he was looking at me and thinking: that guy's doing what he's doing just because it's fun.

Most bird sightings are quick. But this went on. I got a slow look at this badass bird as it lingered over the clearing that it clearly owned.

The fanned out tail was backlit, showing some redness. The wings were wide and flat. The beak, curved and pointed. Talons were tucked-in, weapons not in use for the moment.

I wasn't seeing a lot of birds today, but I was seeing a lot of bird.

Tuesday, July 9

Pitchers and Turkeys

Watching baseball on TV, you think: why does yet another pitcher have an overly long goatee?

The idea hits: Must be a survival adaptation. A major league distraction to the hitter.

Hell, if you're facing a human cannon who's going to fire a hardball 90 miles an hour at you, you don't want to be looking at his weird beard.

But you can't help it. And that throws off your swing.

Several pitchers—too many to be a coincidence—have these big goatees.

This is similar to a survival adaptation on male wild turkeys. You watch these birds in a Wisconsin prairie that's green as a ball diamond this time of year, and you think: what's with the wattles?

Seems that male turkeys, especially when they get aggressive, flaunt these facial blobs under their chins.

The science on this subject says it gives them an advantage in natural selection by intimidating competing males.

Huh. Makes sense. Birds and pitchers both use gimmicks on their faces to get a competitive edge. Smart. A little strange, but smart.

Wednesday, July 3

The F-word

You don't think much of flocking birds. You're a lone hiker, someone who never cared to be part of a crowd.

You stare at a flock of Starlings, a flock of geese, a flock of Cedar Waxwings in a berry tree.

But you don't like that F-word: flock.

That doesn't mean you don't like these birds. Especially the waxwings; they're just damn cool.

But you'd like them better if they had a more independent outlook.

A Bald Eagle circles, aloof, owning his or her sky, and you respect that old bird.

A Red-tailed Hawk stakes out a signpost. Alone, regal, happy. If you think he wants company, just look in his eyes.

When you go into the woods, you go alone. You find your spot. If others enter, you hear them before you see them, and move.

You have nothing against those who flock, birds or people—and part of you understands the need for social and defensive grouping.

But still. You like the birds and the people who don't flock up the woods.

Wednesday, June 26

Creeps

Some birds are creepy.

Not vultures. Vultures are all wingspan, and fun to watch. Not Ravens. Poe gave Ravens a bad rap. Ravens are genius smart, with envious longevity.

No, these creepy birds are in a dead tree, something out of a horror film, hunched, ominous.

But wait......

You've seen these birds flying. Like World War Two aircraft. Sleek and awkward both. Not creepy, when on the wing.

And you've seen them swimming. Like submarines, engineered for stealth. Not creepy, when in the water. So when are they creepy?

When they're sitting still. Watching.

Every year they return to leafless branches above a shallow lake. With jagged beaks and vampire wings these birds look like they migrated from the seventh circle of hell.

Yeah, a dead tree with a Double-crested Cormorant looking down at you is creep city.

Not that you mind. But you gotta call it like it is.

Thursday, June 20

Beer Time

After a presentation to clients, I like to get home in time for a beer or two before dinner. My toast to having made it through another meeting.

Today I broke tradition.

Driving past a vacant lot covered with standing water, I saw a Great Blue Heron. I pulled over and got out my binoculars. They can reveal more than you expect.

I saw that in addition to the heron there were many low-riding ducks. Mallards and teals. And a blue-billed Ruddy Duck in the shallows, lost or crazy.

A single cormorant. Sandpipers on the mud. And a skinny Common Egret, looking like an albino version of the Great Blue Heron.

The thought occurred that maybe Great Blue Herons were meant to be named Gray Blue Herons, but people heard 'great' instead of 'gray' and nobody bothered to correct them. Would have been a more accurate name.

Had to head home. It was getting late and I'd miss out on that leisurely toast of a beer or two before we ate.

Instead, I spent Beer Time watching birds on swampy city land in the late sun. It wasn't bad.

Wednesday, June 12

The quick hike

When writing you can make a point quickly, without piling up a lot of words. I wondered if this economy of time could somehow apply to hiking.

I like to disappear into the woods for hours. But, on days that don't allow enough time for that, I lose out.

Then I thought: hell, sometimes I trim a rambling five-hundred words down to a hundred words, so maybe I could shorten a ramble in the woods, too.

I parked at the trailhead. Walked for five minutes, and for another five stood in the trees, underbrush and quiet.

Saw a Blue-gray Gnatcatcher in there. Small, quick, and a novelty.

Five minutes later, I was on my way out. Total time, fifteen minutes. A quick hike.

I wouldn't want all my hikes to become quick hikes.

But on that busy day—a day that normally would have had no wildness in it—I went into the woods, got honest mud on my boots and saw a Blue-gray Gnatcatcher.

I'll remember that for a long time. Even though the hike was for a short time.

Friday, June 7

Cowbird mystery

This afternoon I saw ten or so cowbirds together. They do okay in spite of an odd approach to reproduction. The female sneaks her egg into the nest of another kind of bird.

Her kid pushes aside the host family's legitimate offspring, gets more food, matures quickly, takes off and never looks back.

Aside from the weirdness of this, there's a mystery...

Having no cowbird role models, how does a new-born cowbird grow up and know that it's supposed to repeat this unusual cycle?

That's strange enough. But today, another mystery came to mind: How do adult cowbirds find each other and flock together like the ones I saw?

Think about it: Every one grew up as an interloper, fed and raised in the family of a towhee, warbler, vireo, sparrow, or some other unrelated bird.

But when each finally left, he or she knew to seek out other cowbirds. How? They all came from different backgrounds.

A mystery of birdland.

Saturday, May 25

Matchless

You don't see people strike matches much any more. When I was little, my dad would light a cigarette even when we were walking in the woods.

I remember hiking with him, and a few steps away, a bit of flame would be there in the foliage for a blink in time as my dad's match flared.

Today I noticed something like that in a tree near my home. We've had a lot of rain, and everything's green. But there was a flash of hot orange in the leaves.

I thought of my dad starting up a cigarette for relaxation back in those days when people smoked and believed it was good for them.

What I saw today was bright and fast. The bird, with patches of red-orange, didn't sit still. It was there for a moment.

Its color wasn't a cigarette being lit, but something just as quick to come and go: an American Redstart. You see these birds passing through around this time of year, around Memorial Day.

Saturday, May 18

Who's what?

Today I watched a couple of Red-headed Woodpeckers working to build a nest in a hole, high up on an old tree.

Good. This is a species that's in decline, officially described as "near threatened." But they haven't been classified as "rare," yet.

What is rare is this: the two birds I saw, one male, the other female, looked exactly alike.

In the bird world, sexes are usually identified by differences in color.

In the people-world we've got all kinds of ways to announce our gender.

Most birds just use color. Like: a male Scarlet Tanager's red; his mate's olive drab. Even Robins have shades of difference. And so on.

But, with Red-headed Woodpeckers there's no way to tell. According to experts, even experts can't do it.

Both sexes are the same size and build, with identical coloration.

So how do the birds know who's what?

This has even stumped the world's greatest know-it-all, the internet.

That's okay. The internet can be stumped, and so can we.

The Red-headed Woodpeckers are the only ones who need to know, and somehow, they do.

Sunday, May 5

Navigators

The trees in May have small movements in them. Most people don't notice, but you do.

They're recurring migratory birds called warblers. And like most things, they have good and bad points.

The bad is their name. It demeans these tough little guys. They don't warble. If they make a sound, it's more of a buzz.

They fly in squadrons for thousands of miles, and are pure stamina. They ought to be called navigators, not warblers.

Yellow Warbler, Prothonotary Warbler, Chestnut-sided Warbler, Blackburnian Warbler, Wilson's Warbler, Tennessee Warbler, Palm Warbler, Hooded Warbler and many more; the warbler family is big.

But the family name's not fair to these athletes. If you were naming a sports team, would you pick: "The Warblers?"

Now, here's what's good about them. Continuity.

Every year, they muscle their way over oceans, lakes, gulfs, rivers, woods, mountains, canyons, forests, through storms, and around tall buildings, only to show up in your backyard for a while.

You can count on them. As warbler seasons pile up behind you, you appreciate that kind of thing.

Tuesday, April 23

Strong

You might think you're strong. You work out. You lifted weights as a kid. And played a lot of sports. But you're a featherweight compared to a Golden Eagle.

You think you're strong enough to drag a 14-foot steel rowboat up a beach. Can't weigh more than 150 pounds, way less than your own weight. So you throw out your back.

("Gotta weak back—when'd ya get it—'bout a week back—slap, smack, bonk." –The Three Stooges, circa 1935.)

Meanwhile, the Golden Eagle has been said to carry off goats and even heavier prey. The bird can lift three times its weight. About 540 pounds, if it were you.

And it's got no problem. No weak back. No week of pain meds just to get out of bed.

Many birds out-muscle us. Ospreys, crows, woodpeckers. To say nothing of Ostriches—which hardly count as birds, but still…

They're all stronger, pound for pound, than we are. Another reason to appreciate watching birds in the wild, even if your hike's cut short because your back is killing you, rowboat boy.

Sunday, April 14

"The grebe is back"

What kind of grebe? C'mon. If somebody says, "The grebe is back," is that the first thing you'd ask?

More likely, you'd say: who is this guy, and what the hell is a grebe?

But wait. You have some interest in birds, so maybe you do wonder what kind of grebe, of all possible grebes, it could be.

We'll get to this grebe's identity. But first, another observation.

In Illinois, American Robins used to be the birds that told us spring was coming. Not any more. Now, they stay through winter. You see them year 'round.

This means little, except that things change.

But grebes don't change. There's a pond here, and every April it's got a grebe in it, meaning that spring has arrived.

Grebe migration is happening. We see it in action by spotting this single grebe. A Pied-billed Grebe, in case you want to know. Since you've read this far, you probably do.

Let's drink to that. Here's to people who want to know about grebes. And things that don't change.

Tuesday, April 9

Time and a favorite bird

Take your kids to Disney World over the years, and they change like time-lapse photography.

This place makes you notice time passing. You also notice birds. Including a favorite, which I'll get to in a minute.

First, quick impressions: A Mockingbird on an umbrella table. A pair of Ospreys hunting over Bay Lake. They don't care if the lake's manmade. Its fish are real.

Anhingas and Double-crested Cormorants are on the shoreline. White Ibises walk among crowds. Long-legged tropical birds acting like pigeons. Goofy.

Black Vultures and Turkey Vultures watch. Maybe a goofy Ibis is dead. Or a feral pig rots in the palmettos. There's a lot to eat at Disney World.

A Wild Turkey walks the golf course. Boat-tailed Grackles are common. American Coots float in Fantasy Land. A Bald Eagle circles above it all.

Then there's an all-time favorite bird. He was around when you were a kid and still is, right on your wrist, keeping the time.

Hi Donald.

Wednesday, March 27

Birds of few words

The terse writer Cormac McCarthy comes to mind. His writing has little excess language. ("No Country for Old Men," "The Road").

I thought about him recently because I got a question about the identity of a tan, black and blue bird seen in the Old World.

Jay, I figured. Just Jay. No excess language needed.

Here in the New World we don't have that kind of simplicity. We have Blue Jays, Steller's Jays, Gray Jays, Scrub Jays.

In Eurasia, just Jay.

According to field guides, many Eurasian birds are commonly known by single names: Nuthatch, Wren, Blackbird, Kingfisher, Teal.

While here, there are White-breasted Nuthatches, Marsh Wrens, Brewer's Blackbirds, Belted Kingfishers, Blue-winged Teals.

Old World birds must have been the originals, first to get named. Our regional variations of these species had to carry further instructions.

Here, we have a Black-billed Cuckoo. And a Yellow-billed one. In Europe they have a Cuckoo. One word.

Such short bird names are good. Easy to read and remember. Like something Cormac McCarthy would write. Enough said.

Thursday, March 14

Hike

It's not just a walk in the wild. It's a football snap. A pay raise. A skirt lifting. Hike is a versatile word.

But, mainly it's a walk in the wild.

You head through deep forest. There's snow in patches and you see tracks. You think about a bobcat.

You get to a river and there's beaver sign, wood shavings. You see Wood Ducks, wildly colored.

Under the roots of a tree is a den. Half-eaten raccoon nearby, its spinal cord pebbly. A coyote lives here, far from the trail.

You bushwhack on. A bird squawks over the water. Belted Kingfisher.

A deer with erect ears is watching you. You watch back. Three other deer become clear. They jump away, white tails up.

You see a Great Horned Owl, tree-colored, in a tree. You're warm in the freezing day, pushing on.

You reach the rapids where water pours over rocks. A few years ago, your dog jumped in and you helped her climb out, both of you soaked.

Here, time stands still. Yet time passes. Maybe the owl understands how both can be true.

Hours later you head out, bushwhacking, still bushwhacking. You think: don't forget this hike. Write it down.

Sunday, March 10

Forget naked

You have binoculars but don't use them. This is known among birders as naked birding. Popular among the confident and complacent.

Example: in a late winter field you see a flock of ground birds in snow and weeds. You know at a glance they're merely Dark-eyed Juncos and House Sparrows.

But a slightly different one catches your eye. You stop, and, okay, you whip out the binoculars.

An early Northern Waterthrush? Ovenbird? Swainson's Thrush? It's reddish—maybe a Wood Thrush?

Focus, man. That's no thrush; it's a Fox Sparrow. A personal favorite, with its streaked front and long tail. Been a while since you've seen one.

Now you're feeling like your old self. Not naked. Not complacent. A little energized.

Every once in a while, you gotta wrap your two fists around a pair of binoculars and get back to being the birdwatcher you started out being.

Forget naked. Hell, you just saw a Fox Sparrow.

Monday, March 4

Snow happens

A few days ago near Chicago, I watched a couple of Mallards in a late winter storm accumulating snow on their heads.

Things change. Used to be ducks went someplace else; now they're here. They weren't freaks of nature. They were just coated in white, tracking through snow toward a feeder meant for other birds.

Weather patterns changed, migration habits changed, the world changed. They were part of it.

Change is a cold fact, and it goes beyond cold ducks.

A guy can see a recent photo of himself that shows what looks like a snowy coating on his head. He's no duck in winter. He's a guy with hair going white.

It's another way the world changes. You can grouse about it, or take it in stride. Nothing will change the fact of change.

You go about your business with snow on your head.

The snow that's on the Mallards' heads will melt away. These ducks will soon be playing in the sun.

But, your snow's staying. The sobering expression "shit happens" doesn't carry half the weight as "change happens."

Tuesday, February 26

Just looking

I flew to New York recently, got a window seat, and as usual, spent most of the flight watching the world below us.

Back in my frequent flyer days, I once told a business buddy not to think of me as an idiot for spending most of the flight looking out of the window instead of talking to him.

He said he did think I was an idiot.

During my stay in New York, I noticed a seagull flying over 8th Avenue and 34th Street. Pretty far from the waterfront.

I couldn't tell what kind of gull it was. Herring? Ring-billed? Something rare? Glaucous, Iceland, Bonaparte's?

Forget it. Just a gull in a gray sky, looking down at the city below. It headed uptown, taking its time, forty stories high.

I don't think it was searching for food on 8th Avenue. It wasn't an idiot. It was just enjoying being above it all, appreciating the view.

Monday, February 18

Unexpected

You think you have to go into wilderness to see wild birds.

Then you drive along an Interstate north of Chicago and see a Bald Eagle fly over your car. Wide black wings. White head. No doubts.

Once again, birds remind you that they're going to be where you find them. Or where they find you.

You could hike through the North Woods. Freeze your butt, tear your pants, twist your knee, and never see a Bald Eagle.

You'd go to wild places anyway. Eagles aren't the only reason. When you're in the wilderness, you're back where you came from. You feel good.

But Interstate highways are also where you came from. They make you feel good, too. They bring you where you want to go. Sometimes they bring you an unexpected sighting.

It's a free country. Why shouldn't this bird be there? Especially this bird.

Wednesday, February 13

Place names

Winter in the woods. There's a small pond just this side of the river. It's flat ice, making you wish you'd brought skates.

At that frozen pond, I saw a Great Blue Heron. It was standing on the hard surface, and didn't look happy.

Next day, it was gone and I never saw it there again.

When I was a kid, my family drove to a state park for a summer vacation. At the entrance, we saw a man lying in weeds. My dad stopped the car and got out. Gotta see if that guy's okay, he said, cigarette dangling.

Just sleepin' the man said.

Through the years, we came back to that state park for other vacations, and always looked for the guy lying at the side of the road.

Every time I hike near the small pond in the woods, I look for the heron I'd seen standing on ice.

If I felt the need to name things, I'd name the pond Heron Pond. And I'd call the road Sleeping Man Road.

But I'm not in the business of naming things. Still, that doesn't stop me from remembering them. And, in a way, that's the same thing.

Thursday, February 7

Viral

On a freezing day, I put an extra amount of seeds in our feeders. Then a bag broke. Pounds of seeds fell to the ground.

So what. It was cold. Birds could use the food.

But by morning, it became clear that this act went viral. Birds came in droves. More noticed, and they came, too. Exponential growth. The ideology of the internet, gone wild.

Juncos, woodpeckers, nuthatches, chickadees, goldfinches, sparrows, doves, waxwings, cardinals, jays.

And squirrels, herds of squirrels.

There's a message here: If you put something into the world that touches the right chord, it gets noticed.

This is not the same as making a video that goes viral, or writing a best seller. Those things are next to impossible. This was just next to a kitchen window.

Still, you know you're responsible. You feel a little funny about having created all that activity. You think, whoa, what did I do?

Sunday, February 3

Shafted

I saw a Canada Goose with an arrow through it. Half coming out one side. Half coming out the opposite side.

The goose was with others, standing in a winter field, looking around, eyes calm, just another day at the office.

The arrow must have hurt. Probably cut down on certain activities. Might've affected the goose's rank in the flock. But he seemed to be getting on with his life.

I figured this odd observation was worth a brief mention. But first I Googled "goose with arrow" to see if it really is odd.

Well, it's odd, okay, but not because it's uncommon. It's odd because it's pretty damn common.

Google pages are full of stories about geese walking, swimming and flying around wearing arrows stuck through them.

These birds are a good example of living with what the universe sends your way. The universe, on the other hand, has some explaining to do.

Thursday, January 24

9 degrees of separation

It's 9 degrees. The wind is bitter. Ice-coated tree branches rattle against each other. None of this should keep you out of the woods.

You like to debunk the bunk that birders can be wimpy. Mostly, birders are rugged hardasses.

Even in winter, you'll often hike through the forest to a riverbank where you hang out. Gotta get into the wild if you want to be where the wildlife is.

But, today an unwelcome inner wimp got the upper hand, convincing you that 9 degrees is too damn cold.

So you stayed in and stayed warm, while you watched birds, separated from you by a picture window.

They were mobbing a backyard feeder. Hairy, Downy and Red-bellied Woodpeckers, Cardinals, a Blue Jay, a Mourning Dove, juncos, winter goldfinches, nut-hatches, chickadees.

Plenty to watch, and pretty interesting. But you have to be honest: this isn't what it's all about. This isn't your brand of bird watching

Thursday, January 17

Woods, not words

Sometimes, you go into the woods to get away from words.

If you deal in words, if you're a writer, a reader or just a listener, words can weigh you down after a while.

You go to the woods not expecting birds, yet there's a cold kingfisher sitting on a bare branch. You and the kingfisher see each other, but keep your thoughts to yourselves.

You come to a small dam where river water pools and spills. Even if somebody came along and said something, you wouldn't hear.

But nobody will come along. You're off the trail, off the grid. Only trees, and the spaces between trees, for as far as you can see.

There are birds. But no words. That's the way you like it, the way you need it on this day.

When you leave the woods, all settled and free of words, what craziness makes you go to the keyboard and type these?

Thursday, January 10

"Man-agement"

Woods. A place away from humans. Bare trees. Frozen undergrowth, deer, mink, coyotes. Birds.

Ironic. You go there to see birds, and the birds are waiting in your backyard. Why would they go into the wilderness where there are no feeders?

But, maybe you'll spot something too wild for feeders. Maybe a White-winged Crossbill, rumored to be in the area. That would be a first.

You see a manmade sign. "Deer Management Area." You translate this bullshit: "Deer Killing Area."

Killing, also called "culling," is done for reasons of population ecology.

Years ago, local activists mounted an ad campaign around the slogan, "Fighting for deer life." Clever words did nothing to stop the man in management.

Again, sharpshooters wait to cull.

Sharpshooter is a word thought by some to originate from the Sharps Rifle, a long-range gun introduced in the 1800s.

Words. Sharpshooter. Culling. Killing. Management. You walk past the sign and sit by an unfrozen river in the trees.

If there are fewer deer, well, maybe you'll see a White-winged Crossbill. If you don't, there's still the river. They haven't managed that yet.

Thursday, January 3

Belly

You saw a Red-bellied Woodpecker on a nearby branch. Almost close enough to touch. You figure you'll tell somebody.

But the word "bellied" stops you.

This woodpecker stands out because it has a bright red head. But, it can't be called a "Red-headed Woodpecker." Another bird already grabbed that name.

Still, red-bellied?

Any trace of redness that might or might not be on this bird's belly is no reason to name the whole bird after it.

And belly is a childish word. This woodpecker's a heavy-hitter. With a jackhammer beak and a red football helmet.

You want to say: hey, a Red-bellied Woodpecker on a branch was real close. Something to see. But you don't.

Anybody you tell this to will be thinking about bellies. So you don't say anything.

Tuesday, December 18

Streak

A Cooper's Hawk tore past my windshield. It was going too fast to identify. That's how I identified it.

You might ask: how can you say it wasn't a Sharp-shinned Hawk? Northern Harrier? A Peregrine? But if you know Cooper's Hawks, you wouldn't ask this.

It dropped over the treetops on my right, sped downward and crossed the road, disappearing into the tree line on my left with no slowing, just confidence.

I once saw a coyote chase down a rabbit. I used to think my dog was fast when I watched her running in a park. But, that was child's play. A coyote has a whole different kind of speed.

Wild things can be wildly fast.

And this Cooper's Hawk drove that point home while I was driving home. If it caught a bird on the wing after shooting in front of me, I didn't see.

But its success as a hunter is self-evident. Otherwise, it couldn't be this streak of muscle and talons, a living warplane that tears into its prey after tearing ass into the woods.

Friday, December 14

Still

You walk a trail on a December afternoon. It's cold and getting dark. Bare trees stand still. You lean on one. Like hanging out on a street corner, watching the world go by.

Your dad said he wanted to stand "by the side of the road and be a friend to man," paraphrasing dead poet Sam Walter Foss. Your dad, an uneducated guy, could surprise you that way.

All you want to do is stand by the side of the trail. Forget man.

A White-winged Crossbill could change this day. But it doesn't show up. Mink live here. Why doesn't one move? The river's not far. Once, a beaver the size of a pig walked across the trail and didn't hurry on your account.

But today, this place is a still photograph.

No geese or lines of Sandhill Cranes overhead. No Brown Creepers. Nothing. You're the last living being on the planet. You stand in the trees, and the trees stand and do nothing.

But you stay, still, in a still photo that's not a photo, but the only world you've got on this day. And you like it, still.

Saturday, December 8

Crowded

I went to a nature preserve and got off the trail. December's great; no bugs, no people.

I bushwhacked through tall grass, climbed over deadfall and went deep into the woods. Everything was quiet, including me.

I leaned against a tree and waited. Maybe I'd see birds. Maybe deer, a coyote, a fox. Once I saw a Woodcock walk through leaf litter around here.

Nothing. A long stretch of nothing.

But, there's never really nothing in the woods. There's the satisfying smell of wet ground.

A comfortable solitude.

And timelessness. It could have been today, or a thousand years ago.

Wait: I caught a speck of blue off in the distance.

Awright, I figured, maybe a Blue Jay. One of my favorites.

It was far away. Barely visible through the trees. I aimed my binoculars, scanned and focused.

There. It's a guy in a blue hat, moving on the trail I'd left a while back. What the hell? The Blue Jay turned out to be a hat.

I moved on, further into the trees to a different part of the forest, where it wasn't so damn crowded.

Tuesday, November 27

Rarity

You saw a pigeon. Also known as a "Rock Dove," if you want to get dweeby about it.

You're in a wild prairie, far from any city.

Tall, dead weeds blow in the November cold. Deer bed down in them. You see the mashed areas, looking like crop circles. But they're not alien-made.

The only aliens in this prairie are you—and the pigeon.

You've seen Goldfinches here. A Kestrel. A befuddled Bluebird that should've migrated. White-crowned Sparrows, Dark-eyed Juncos, various woodpeckers in the nearby woods, but nothing Pileated.

Unusual birds aren't the reason for coming. You're here for open air, solitude and timeless terrain.

You rarely see a rarity. (A Horned Lark, once).

Then: This lone pigeon flies over the weeds and lands nearby. A bird of city pavement, trainyards, rooftops, alleys, defaced statues. Not the wild prairie.

So you look. And you figure, hey, a rarity. Once again, a hike in the outdoors has come through for you.

Wednesday, November 21

Inordinate fondness

The naturalist J. B. S. Haldane famously said, "The Creator has an inordinate fondness for beetles."

There are more species of these bugs than any other animal on earth—nearly 400,000.

Haldane might also have said the Creator has a fondness for Red-tailed Hawks on highway lampposts and power-line poles.

Today I averaged seeing more than one Red-tail per mile on the busy expressway system that winds around and through Chicago.

Hell, you could walk around in the great open wilderness until a few thousand beetles eat you, and still not see any hawks.

But they're on urban, suburban and exurban highway poles in inordinate numbers.

Nothing like the number of beetle species. But still, the Haldane quote comes to mind.

All these big, heavy bodied, fierce-eyed, roadside hawks, more than one per highway mile.

I don't know about the Creator, but I gotta say, I've got a fondness for them.

They make the road a little more interesting.

If you don't believe this, next time you're driving the freeways, look up.

Wednesday, November 14

A lot of nuthatches

I'm seeing Red-breasted Nuthatches a lot. That's something you don't say to just anyone.

Wouldn't have said it to high school buddies. Wouldn't say it in a business meeting, no matter how friendly the suits might be.

Hell, I don't think I'd say it over dinner with friends, even after a few drinks. You start talking about nuthatches, people start thinking you're one.

But I'd say it to a birdwatcher. I'd say it to you.

Small grayish birds with ruddy fronts and striped heads are showing up in woods and backyards way more than usual this November.

I thought maybe it was just me. Maybe I was getting it wrong, oddly imagining a nuthatch population explosion.

So I searched the web before going any further with this.

Yeah, there it was: a story that says nuthatch populations are way up this year.

Nobody knows why. I don't care. At least I'm not nuts. There are a lot of nuthatches out there, and I'm seeing them.

Thursday, November 8

Intrusion

The November wilds. Woods, fields, a muddy riverbank, nothing manmade. It's a good time of year. Few bugs, few leaves. Solitude.

There are Dark-eyed Juncos, drab American Goldfinches. A grayish Eastern Bluebird. Cedar Waxwings. Coyote scat with rabbit fur.

A big hawk lands high on a bare tree. It fans a reddish tail. A Red-tailed Hawk, right?

But no. It has blue markings. Bright blue.

I try to get a better look but it takes off. Gone. A hawk I can't identify.

Later I ask the guru, Google: "red-tail hawk with color on wings."

Mystery solved. Scientists near O'Hare are hawk tagging. Stapling bright ID's onto wings for study purposes.

I guess the taggers have good reasons. But, that colorful tag is an intrusion. A bit of the manmade where it doesn't belong.

And if I think that, imagine what the hawk thinks.

Thursday, October 25

The enemy of bird watching

That old four-letter word. Work.

On days when I would've been near the river looking at a Belted Kingfisher...on days when I would've stood in weeds watching a Pine Siskin...I've been working.

On days when I'd have been looking at beaver dams, coyote tracks, or watching deer turn and watch me right back...I've been working.

Or...when I'd glass a Red-tailed Hawk only to find it's an Osprey...when I'd see an Eastern Bluebird and think: that'd be corny if it weren't real...

On those days, I've been working.

Yeah, don't complain. Many want work and can't find it. Been there myself. Work has good points, but it's also the enemy of bird watching.

Instead of getting tired in fresh air, I've been getting tired in office buildings. Inside looking out. What the hell, man?

Time to get back to the lone prairie and wooded trail. Work's good. But c'mon, you gotta have your priorities.

Wednesday, October 10

Birdland

I go into the wild on a freezing fall morning. To distract me from the cold wind, I find myself whistling "Lullaby of Birdland." A bluesy old tune by George Shearing.

I spot a sparrow with a streaked chest. Teddy Roosevelt knew this bird without seeing it. He once picked up a feather and said, "Hmm, Fox Sparrow."

I hike on, whistling.

I see a Yellow-rumped Warbler at the edge of the woods. "Hey, Myrtle," I say. A joke between me, the bird, and anyone who doesn't like names that change.

Over an open field, two uncommon Broad-winged Hawks are circling, part of the migration.

After watching them for a while, I enter a canopy of colorful trees. Near a small river I see a Belted Kingfisher. A black-belt. He's fishing and doesn't care that I'm there.

I'm warm now, and undo my coat. "Lullaby of Birdland" is still on my mind. Birdland's a jazz club in New York. All the greats played there.

Birdland is also where I'm hanging out today. All the greats play here, too.

Friday, October 5

Doorstep

There was an unusual bird on my doorstep this morning.

The word doorstep is broadly used to mean "right under your nose." So, you might think the unusual bird wasn't on my actual doorstep, and I was using the word symbolically.

No. These notes are nothing if not true.

Through the glass panel alongside my front door I saw the unusual bird next to our welcome mat.

It was poking at a wrinkled worm.

In the house, I slowly knelt. The bird was right on the other side of the glass.

I got a close-up view of its eye stripe. Streaked chest. Two-tone browns.

After a while, I had to take off. I opened the door, and the Northern Waterthrush took off, too, all part of the fall migration.

I'd been wanting to get into the wild with boots, binoculars, and time to spare, but had been putting it off.

No problem. Sometimes you go to the birds; sometimes they go to you.

Wednesday, September 26

Vegas gnatcatcher

I have a friend: Ex-army, ex-newsman, horseplayer, craps-shooter, crime novelist, two-fisted drinker.

A guy who would've loved a night on the town with Bogart, Spillane and some dames.

He just spent a few days in Vegas, and writes that he saw a gnatcatcher there. Huh?

I wouldn't have guessed he'd know a gnatcatcher from a dogcatcher.

Such is the rise of modern bird watching. Something we can all be proud of.

There are two kinds of gnatcatchers in Nevada. Blue-gray and Black-tailed.

I saw a Blue-gray in a prairie north of Chicago this year. Not an everyday bird.

I joked to my wife that I wished we had a pet gnatcatcher because we had gnats. Those suckers bite, leaving red bumps in the night.

Maybe you can't have a gnatcatcher as a pet. But it's good to spot one in the wild. Like my friend did, near Vegas.

I don't care that he didn't specify which of the two it was. I'm just glad he used the word "gnatcatcher." That's worth writing home about.

Thursday, September 20

Pelicans

Pelicans are funny looking on land. Then they fly and they're... beautiful. Look at a pelican on the wing and tell me I'm wrong.

I knew a former Golden Gloves boxer, an old-timer.

He was not great looking out of the ring. He'd got bald and had a belly.

One day, I watched him teaching a kid some boxing moves. It was...beautiful.

He had that uncanny left-right coordination that the great athletes have.

When he shadow-boxed, he fit into his own skin like a glove. Boxing transformed him; it was something he was meant to do.

Just like flying is something a pelican was meant to do. When you see one of these portly, jowly birds on a pier, don't write him off.

Wait'll you see him fly. That's how to appreciate him, along with some people you might know.

Saturday, September 15

Five minutes

Minute one: Looking for a few minutes of warmth, and nothing more, I go to the shore of a small lake. My only interest is sun, which is strong there.

Minute two: A big bird comes over the trees then curves out of sight. Red-tailed Hawk? Turkey Vulture? Can't get a good look. Forget it.

Minute three: It comes back, and comes close. An Osprey. Its wings have bent front edges. Bent like knees, if wings had knees. That wing shape means: "Osprey." Ospreys are not common. Must be part of the fall migration.

Minute four: The Osprey flies over me, low. I get a good look. It's holding a fish. Probably looking for a dead tree where it can alight and eat. Trees above me are thick with leaves. The Osprey leaves.

Minute five: I think about how you could spend five hours looking for an unusual bird. And, in five minutes there's an Osprey, here and gone.

Dumb luck is quick, and cannot be underestimated.

Wednesday, September 12

Next time

A Great Blue Heron flew over an expressway north of Chicago today. It reminded me of a similar heron, seen at another place and time.

The other heron was standing in a beachside park near Tarpon Springs, Florida, and was unfazed as I approached.

He stared at me and held his ground.

These birds are incorrectly named blue. But correctly named great. I'd have gone with "Spear-faced Heron."

I had brought a bag of McDonald's to the beach, and was in a mood to share. I thought I'd toss a burger to the heron.

But I didn't. Figured it might be bad to interfere with the circle of life, some bullshit like that. Stupid.

Any bird living on raw frogs and fish would've liked an all-beef patty.

When today's Great Blue flew over my car, I thought: if I ever see you on the ground around here, and if I've got a bag of burgers…

Saturday, September 8

Bridge

Silly hats worn at both political conventions show that tribalism can make people look foolish.

Better are those who run with no tribe, the lone wolves. Daniel Boone, Thoreau, Ed Abbey. (Forget Boone's silly hat).

The thought of being a lone wolf reminded me of an incident...

I was on a wooden footbridge over a creek in deep woods, taking a break. I'd hiked in for solitude, but also for the birds.

Saw a Northern Flicker, no rarity but a favorite. Fall warblers. An Ovenbird, a reddish Wood Thrush.

I'd been leaning on the railing, unmoving, when a coyote walked into the creek bed below, not knowing I was there.

He kept coming, then looked up and stopped.

A long moment of eye contact. Then, he went on his way without hurrying or looking back, dignity intact.

Later, while watching conventioneers on TV, I thought about lone wolves, having seen the real deal that day.

And I said to myself: gotta get back to that bridge.

Monday, September 3

Molt

A male Scarlet Tanager kicks ass all summer.

Its wild coloration defies camouflage and common sense. Hot red. Black wings. As if designed by an artist who's high.

But, now, in September it changes from gaudy to drab.

This bright bird—a bird that stood out like a stop sign in the woods—goes from red to yellow-green.

It molts. Not a nice word: molt. Molting is another measure of time slipping into the future.

It makes September more than a month, but a metaphor. As the days grow short, look how your hair goes gray. Or goes away.

But a tanager's molt, unlike ours, is temporary.

The bird flies to a jungle for the winter. When it reappears it's hot red again, and red hot.

Maybe that's why we search for tanagers in spring. Nice to see that some things can come back.

Saturday, August 25

Bookstore gulls

The bookstore is a two-story dinosaur, counting days until the web nudges it aside.

Meanwhile, web feet are in its parking lot.

The place has no water. No garbage. Just cars in the hot sun. Yet, every signpost has a gull on it.

Ring-billed. Or Herring. Or both. Maybe a rare Thayer's. The differences are subtle.

You came for a book, not bird watching. But, what the hell. You look at the gulls.

There's a two-story bookstore in a different mall. It recently closed. A monument to the twin partners of progress and extinction.

There are no gulls in that shuttered store's empty parking lot. They don't go there any more. No one does.

As you stand in the parking lot of the bookstore that's still alive, you try to pick out Ring-billed from Herring, and you look for Thayer's.

But you don't really care what these gulls are called. You're just glad they're not out of business.

Wednesday, August 22

"Bird"

There was a time.

Jazz played on the radios of nighttime cars with steamed-up windows, cars with steamed-up couples parked for romance.

The music was part of the mood. And the memory. Coltrane, Miles Davis. Charlie Parker.

Parker was a saxophone player nicknamed "Bird." One of his albums is even titled, "Ornithology."

There was a night when, above Parker's sax on the car radio, I heard another cool sound.

In the old trees above our parked car was an owl. I cared.

I remember trying to concentrate on other things, but couldn't help thinking: Great Horned? Maybe Barn?

Great Horned won the guessing game with a smile because of the great horniness in our world at that time and place.

But, a better sound than even that of a wild owl in a wild tree came from Parker's wild sax.

Part of the sound track of that night. Charlie Parker. Another bird for your life list.

Saturday, August 18

The unclassified bird

It's you. Impossible to pigeonhole.

Maybe you're the guy who looks like a kickass biker. Handlebar moustache. Sitting on a hog.

Your interests include Nascar and opera. Wait: opera? And you like Seinfeld reruns. Huh?

Maybe you're the lady feeding hummingbirds. Gotta be a grandma who knits, right? No. You're a cop.

People, in general, defy stereotyping. But here and now, we're talking about wildlife observers. Birdwatchers. You.

You're young. You're old. Male, female, rural, urban. Burly, frail, sexy, unsexy.

High-IQ, average IQ, underestimated IQ. You might wear a suit and tie. Or no shoes.

Like birds, you come in many colors. Unlike birds, you couldn't be put into a field guide.

You might look like you can be figured out based on where you live, how you dress or talk, things like that.

But you're not so easy to classify. That's a fact of nature, and it's one of the best.

Sunday, August 12

Parking like a cop

I'm driving a wooded road near here, and a bird rises from the foliage. I'd know that white rump anywhere.

Flickers have been strangely scarce this summer.

I quickly turn into the roadside weeds, diagonally, and stop. This violates our rules of the road. What the hell.

I hike toward the trees, but the Flicker's gone.

Funny, all these years liking that bird, spotting it in its various forms—yellow-shafted, red-shafted, gilded—I never registered that its name is significant.

Until it flashed in front of my car. And disappeared, as I parked like a cop at a bank robbery.

Maybe guys like me who stop for a quick look at wildlife should have flashing lights for their cars.

Couldn't be blue or red. Police and fire have those, and you're not supposed to impersonate. Yellow's taken by road crews.

I guess green would make sense. A flashing green light to slap on your roof. But I don't have one.

Meanwhile, there's a Flicker in the vicinity. If I see it again, watch out for my car.

Saturday, August 4th

Under Sirius

Dog days mean mostly shorebirds. An egret this morning. Listless ducks. Cormorants.

Not a lot overhead.

Except in the night sky before dawn, when Sirius, the Dog Star, is up there. It has given this season its name. Dog days.

Even in this quiet time, there's always something to watch for.

There are reports of a cougar in suburban Chicago. Better to call it a mountain lion. Cougar has come to mean a horny, mid-life woman. That wouldn't be news.

But a mountain lion, now, that makes up for the birds going silent.

The wild has got plenty of things up its sleeve. A West Nile mosquito, carrying imported danger. A skunk under your porch, smelling like raw coffee.

Hell, maybe a bear is walking down your street.

They say there are no bears in Illinois. But, if a lion can cross the state line, so can a bear. Anything's possible while the Dog Star shines.

Scarce birds are okay during the dog days, because we might see a cougar if we're lucky.

I mean, mountain lion.

Saturday, July 28

Ani

An Ani is without doubt a rare bird. I saw one variety, a Smooth-billed Ani, on an island off Florida a while back.

But I haven't seen much around here recently, rare or not.

There's a bird drought in the Midwestern wilds. Still, it's good to check out the wilderness. The woods, ponds and fields.

A friend says you can get hooked on real and metaphoric wilderness. Not sure what the hell he means. Besides, metaphoric is an indoor word. I'd rather be outside.

And hooked is about escapism, I guess. Nothing wrong with a little escapism.

Even though it's a slow season, there have been phoebes near a pond, and mergansers with their ducklings. Also, chickadees, goldfinches, kestrels.

And a big grackle that's not usually here. It looked like an Ani, but without the bulked-up beak.

Beaks are big with Anis. There's the Smooth-billed Ani kind that I mentioned. Also a Groove-billed variety.

The Grackle reminded me of having seen that Ani on the island off Florida. A little avian money in the bank for days when birds are scarce.

Saturday, July 21

News break

After a day of non-stop TV reports, you go to a quiet woodland lake, alone.

You need a break from the violent craziness that media people privately call "good TV."

But, what about violence found in this wild place? Tooth and claw, all that?

Hell, it's here. I've seen a Red-tailed Hawk land on a pheasant in a field nearby, and pull that living bird apart.

Just food. Brutal food, though not crazy. The crazy stuff comes from humans.

Last year, I saw a snake coiled on the road that runs along this lake. A muscle car sped past, then stopped. The driver slammed into reverse, running his tires back over the snake.

I said to him, a guy with tattooed arms in a cutoff shirt, "What the hell?" He answered, "Read your bible, asshole, they're evil."

Then peeled out, leaving blood, guts and snakeskin.

Okay, back to the small, woodland lake for whatever middling, mid-summer bird life might be seen around sunset. Not much.

But it's good to be in a place where there's no television, no news, and no people.

Thursday, July 19

Hobo

They call such a bird a vagrant. But I prefer hobo. An old word that means carefree wanderer.

The sighting that's causing these thoughts is an improbable Tri-colored Heron. A bird not found in Chicago.

But I saw one in a pond near a highway cloverleaf around here. Looked like a Great Blue, but brown. And smaller.

Tri-colored Herons live in the southeast.

But, today, I saw it again. Could be an American Bittern, I thought. Bitterns aren't lanky, though. This was lanky. Like a Great Blue, but brown.

Done: I'm going with Tri-colored. No range map is going to stop me. Birds fly. Western Tanagers from Colorado have been known to surprise people in New England.

And if a 300-pound Jaguar can wander from Mayan jungles to Texas, a bird can be anywhere.

Tri-colored Heron. It was near a Chicago highway, and I saw it. A genuine vagrant, one for the record books.

Or, to put it more simply, a non-conformist hobo living a life free of maps.

Wednesday, July 11

Look up

You might think every wild bird is extinct. It's mid-summer, dead quiet.

But, there are House Wrens nesting secretly in my basketball hoop. Near a pond today I happened to see an Eastern Phoebe catching bugs from a branch, working without a sound.

On the way to a business meeting I passed a lifeless tree out of Poe. It had ghoulish Double-crested Cormorants looking down on our traffic.

At a wedding Sunday, a Red-tailed Hawk circled. Nobody seemed to notice. Later, a quiet Kestrel blended into a telephone pole.

A lone Blue-winged Teal flew like a bat out of hell in a place where there was no water. The duck was unseen, as far as I could tell.

Tomorrow could be another birdless day.

But the cormorants will be there, watching people drive past. A Red-tailed Hawk will probably be circling.

Look up. Maybe you'll see them looking down on you.

Thursday, July 5

Jaguar

Some birders drop everything to go after rare birds. These people are tough and dedicated. I'm not one of them.

But I would take a trip to see a jaguar.

I've been reading frontier tales. In one, Comanches found a jaguar in south Texas.

I checked the internet for modern jaguar sightings, and discovered that they've occurred recently on our side of the Mexican border.

I think I'd go there to see a Jaguar. A big jungle cat that wandered into mountain lion territory. Just throw binoculars into the jeep and head out.

There are birds, too, in that wild country. Like Trogons. But they wouldn't be the main attraction.

If that makes me less of a birdwatcher, so be it.

Bird watching isn't always about birds, but it's always about watching.

I'd go there to spot a spotted cat.

Friday, June 29

Woodpecker toes and vodka

I was staring at a Downy Woodpecker's feet today. They brought to mind the memory of a business meeting…

I was in an ad agency, presenting a campaign about golf clubs. The boardroom was filled with smart, tough suits.

To dampen nerves caused by such presentations, I might have sipped a little vodka before going on.

When talking about the importance of stance in golf, I mentioned woodpecker feet. On a vodka-fueled roll, this seemed entirely reasonable.

I pointed out that these peckers have two toes forward, and two back, unlike typical birds that have three forward, one back.

This two-two arrangement gives balance, relating, of course, to golf. Blank stares. I was only saved from the firing squad because the ads were cool.

I still think woodpecker toes are interesting. But I don't plan to talk about them, or any bird parts, in business meetings.

Even if, under certain circumstances, it seems entirely reasonable.

Monday, June 25

Woodpecker thoughts

Maybe something's on your mind. So you go to the woods, away from it all.

You see two woodpeckers on the same tree, and they take hold of your thoughts.

One is a Downy. The other, a Hairy. The Downy's not downy and the Hairy's not hairy. Birds are saddled with stupid names.

But, it gets weirder. These two are different species, yet identical except for size.

Picture it this way:

Look in the mirror. See your face, features, clothing? Now imagine someone joins you, same face, features and clothing. But a foot taller.

The big stranger says to the mirror, "Hey, me and mini-me."

That's what it's like with Hairy and Downy Woodpeckers. Me and mini-me.

You have to wonder what they think about each other. But, maybe they don't think anything about each other and their similarity.

Maybe they just think about bugs in bark.

Yet, you think about it. And while you do, you're not thinking about anything else.

Wednesday, June 13

This is cuckoo

I have a basketball hoop on the garage. Not much keeps my shots from going in.

It's unlikely that something four inches tall could block me. But that's what's happening.

My basket has a wren in it, and every time I toss even a lay-up, the bird pops out.

My backboard is like a cuckoo clock, although the bird's a House Wren, not a cuckoo.

I've seen cuckoos in the woods. Twelve-inch long Yellow-billed Cuckoos, mainly. None of them would want to live under a basket.

But a wren would. It's got a nest in a gap below the hoop. I checked. There's straw.

Now I can't shoot baskets without imagining the thundering shaking that my shots cause. So I don't shoot.

I look at my basketball on the driveway. I look at the orange rim. Weather's good, and the NBA finals are going on. I want to play ball.

But a bird has blocked me. A feisty wren. It may not be a cuckoo. But the situation is pretty cuckoo.

Monday, May 7

Red dot

When I first saw a Downy Woodpecker, I pictured somebody dipping a thumb into red paint and dabbing it on the bird's head, giving it an unexpected spot.

I thought of this when somebody dipped a thumb into red paint and dabbed it on my forehead.

I was at a Hindu wedding, an affair more colorful than my woods in May with their Scarlet Tanagers, Indigo Buntings, Yellow Warblers and Rose-breasted Grosbeaks.

At the wedding I learned that the forehead dot is applied to men as well as women. It's said to signify peace and protection.

Okay, I thought, peace and protection are always in short supply. I bent forward, and a tanager of a woman in a scarlet sari touched a paint-dripping red thumb to my forehead.

I guess I felt a little peaceful and protected for a while. I didn't want to wash off the dot, but it went away anyway.

Next time I see a Downy Woodpecker I'll appreciate his, and remember mine.

About the Author

Mike Lubow is a former VP Creative Director of a multi-national ad agency and founder of a mid-sized Chicago ad agency. (Actually, not mid-sized. Smallish, really, but big of heart).

He's written a popular column called "Got a Minute" for the Chicago Tribune, and has published fiction and non-fiction in a variety of national magazines from the literary to the glossy, some in Australia, New Zealand and several European countries. One of his stories was translated into four other languages.

His newspaper columns have been collected in the book "In a Chicago Minute," and ten of his published short stories have been collected in the book "Paper and Ink." Both books are available online or through bookstores. He's also creator of the online magazine "Two-Fisted Birdwatcher."

The author lives in the Chicago area. He's a husband, father, grandfather, and could've played pro basketball if he were only a little taller.

Acknowledgements

The writing in "Wild Notes" originated within the "Daily Sightings" category of the online magazine "Two-Fisted Birdwatcher." While the pieces in this book represent a lifelong interest in birds and a desire to escape as often as possible to the wild corners of the natural world, they could never have happened without modern technology.

I was encouraged by my tech-savvy offspring to "build a blog" as an outlet for my musings about nature and life. The WordPress platform made this possible with little technical demands on this non-technical guy, and was facilitated by the always patient techie, Adrian Gershom.

My novelist pal Marc Davis set an example by showing that the desire to write means nothing unless you put what you write out there for the world to see. Kathy Smith and Aaron Vargas were essential for book design.

But none of this writing and publishing would have come about if a cute girl I met in college hadn't said she preferred to date creative guys, as well as guys who liked to hike. I started writing to impress her (the hiking was already a habit). She was encouraging back then. Today, as my wife, she still is. Without that, and her proofreading advice, this book wouldn't have happened.

CPSIA information can be obtained
at www.ICGtesting.com
Printed in the USA
FSOW03n2023221216
28771FS